Memoirs Of An Amnesiac

a play by Stan's Cafe

ISBN 978-1-913185-13-8

Published by Stan's Cafe
Birmingham, UK
2020

www.stanscafe.co.uk

Contents:

MEMOIRS OF AN AMNESIAC

new music/theatre by stan's cafe

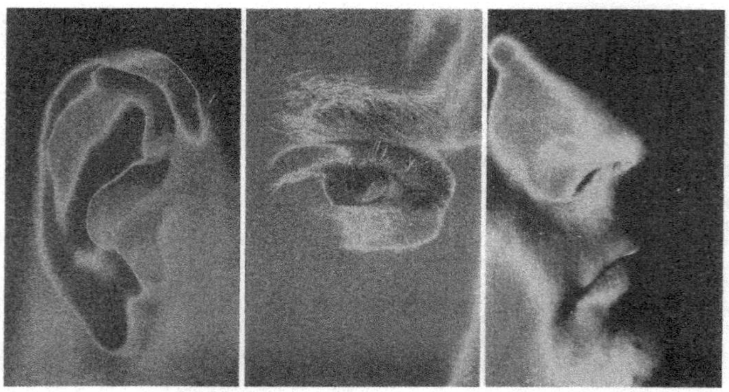

sounds·Erik Satie·Richard Chew·
actions·Graeme Rose·
directions·James Yarker·

Introduction

Memoirs Of An Amnesiac is set in the bed-sit of Eric Smith.

On stage only one corner of his room is visible. It has a door fitted with bolts and a chain. There is a window covered with curtains. A pathetic star mobile is attached to the outside of the window in such a way that if the window is opened the stars disappear. Nothing else can be seen outside. A small phallic cactus sits on the window sill.

The walls are white but stained. There is a fragment of a low ceiling in the corner. On the wall between window and door there is a plain medicine cabinet with two doors that hinge outwards. Other furniture includes a desk (which doubles as a bed), an old school chair, a small cabinet in which is hidden a projector and telephone. A desk lamp sits on the cabinet.

An upright piano stage right completes the room's furnishings.

Smith himself is charmingly nervous, infuriating, pedantic and empathic. He wears an old suit, shirt and black tie, braces and, on occasions, a bowler hat. He smiles like Erik Satie.

Lighting is bold and expressionistic, including the use of a bare hanging bulb and desk light. A pianist plays the piano, taped music and text are delivered over the theatre's speakers.

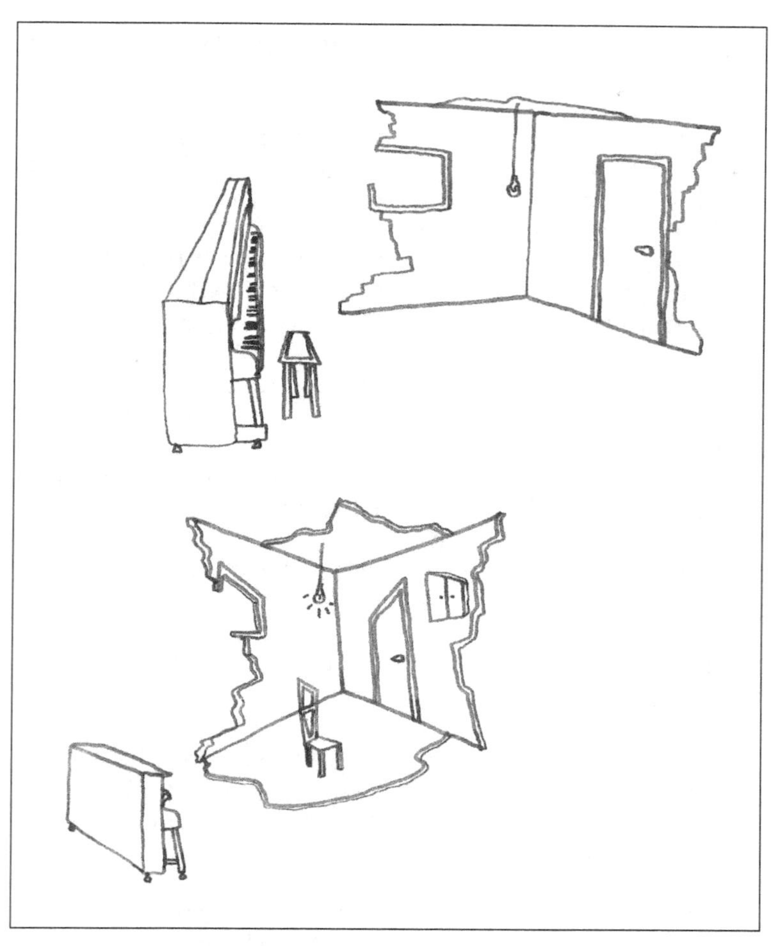

Set sketches by Graeme Rose.

Overture

Opening Chorale plays over speakers.
House lights fade to black.

Eric Smith's voice plays from the speakers whilst the empty set changes character under cross-faded lighting states.

Voice: The writing of a biography necessitates a great deal of painstaking research. When the subject is long dead this research is generally restricted to documents surviving from that person's life, their letters, manuscripts and writings.

Beyond this direct evidence there lies the evidence of biographers who have proceeded you, their insights and false assumptions. This is as far as biographical research generally goes, but for this work I have endeavoured to take evidence from the fragmentary traces a genius always leaves behind when passing on from one world into the next.

Accordingly, I would like to thank the Satie Archivist at the Biblioteque Nationale in Paris for his helpful letter. The authors of those other biographies, my colleagues for their patient understanding, my secretary for her tireless and devoted work transcribing my innumerable redrafts but most of all I must thank the minimalist maestro himself: Erik Satie.

Signed: Eric Smith, Birmingham 1992.

Part 1: The Room

Sonatine Bureaucratique is played by Pianist.

Eric Smith enters.

Part 1 is built on cycles of humdrum actions. These actions work with fragments of Satie's piano music. The relationship between the music and action is constantly shifting, what is cuing what never stabilises. A sense of order is built up and broken down. There is a progression in Smith's mental state.

<u>First Cycle.</u>
Setting up a sense of daily routine.

Enter. Close door.
File down on table.
Shake jacket and throw on chair, then adjust it.
Move to mug on cabinet.
[Blackout]

Sitting at table, back to audience.
Stamp on envelope and seal, put in file.
File in draw.
[Voice starts]
Yawn.
First of facial exercises.
Go to look out of window. Pricked by cactus.
Look outside window.
Get washing kit. Leave.
[Blackout]

Voice: Satie is standing, Debussy is sitting. Satie's left elbow is resting on the back of Debussy's chair, his hand relaxed. His fingers, slightly splayed, must just be touching Debussy's shoulder. Satie has a long waistcoat on, he looks slightly portly, his suit is black, jacket hangs open. His hair though still dark is receding. He has a cigarette in his mouth. This is the only photo in existence of Satie smoking, there is no literary reference to him smoking, thus it would seem reasonable to conclude that he was smoking here for a bet and this photo is the evidence which will enable him to claim his money. In his right hand is an object that cannot be identified I will return to this matter later...

Enter drying self.
Push table to wall to become a bed.
Sleep on table.
[Blackout]

Wake on floor. Move table. Get file.
Put on jacket. Look out of window.
Exit.
[Blackout]

Second Cycle.
A growing sense of nervousness with the outside world and a feeling that whilst being in his room is better than outside, there is something not quite right with the room. Smith mutters to himself.

Enter. Close door.
Mock surprise and excitement at finding a letter.
File and letter down on table.
Shake jacket too much, throw on chair and adjust.
Add letter to pile on piano.
Move to mug.
[Blackout]

Stamping and sealing two envelopes.

Letter in file, file in draw.
Mime piano playing on table. Yawn.
Pull faces at audience.
[Blackout]

Doing bending exercises Smith feels a sudden
shock of pain.
Take crushed can from his trouser pocket.
Put can on piano, unsatisfactory, put it in medicine
cabinet.
Happy with treasure (can). Unhappy going for wash.
[Blackout]

Standing gazing round side of curtain until he
suddenly realises the time.
Grabbing file and jacket go to window.
Pricked by cactus. Glance round edge of curtains.
Worried about exit.
Exit.
[Blackout]

<u>Third Cycle.</u>
Smith is getting decidedly agitated, the outside is
getting more oppressive, inside he is mostly content
but there is a sense of impending crisis.

Enter. Close door (which is a relief).
Find two letters with mock surprise.
Add letters and ear piece to medicine cabinet.
File on desk.
Shake jacket too much, throw at chair, miss.
Pick up jacket, shake too much, throw at chair, miss.
Put jacket on chair, uneasy.
[Blackout]

Stamping and sealing three envelopes, put in file.
Yawn.
Telephone rings.

Panic, check the door is closed, he is smart, the
room is tidy.
Go to answer phone, it stops ringing. Frustrated.
[Blackout]

Distracted, put file and mug in desk draws.
Push table to be bed. Moving chair to wrong place.
Lie down but cannot sleep.
Chair moved to the correct position. Sleep comes.
[Blackout]

Fall off table. Leap up awake.
Move table. Prick self on cactus.
Glance round edge of curtains. To door.
Remember to get file, to door.
Remember to go to window, prick self.
Glance outside.
Exit.
[Blackout]

Fourth Cycle

Smith's smooth routine is breaking down, further
evidence of the room's disturbing nature and the
growing distance from the outside world.

Enter. Grateful to close door.
Look down to be surprised by letters, there are no
letters.
Find letters in file, pretend to pick them up and be
surprised.
Count letters into piano.
Put down file. Go to take off jacket. Realise jacket
was never on.
Put on jacket, pick up file, stand at door.
Close eyes to rerun entry.
Got to take off jacket, realise that the file has not
been put down.
Return to door, close eyes tc re-run entry.

Put down file. Take off jacket, place it on chair.
Go for mug, find it's not there.
Search for mug, find it in draw. Confusion.
[Blackout]

Smith: *[Sitting on table]* Yes, she works on the
            ground floor and I work on the third floor,
            that's where all the work that I do is done,
            so we don't see each other that often;
            that is unless we happen to bump into
            each other on the stairwell, if I'm going
            down to the basement where the
            photostat machine is and if she is going
            up to the second floor. That's where her
            friends work, on the second floor. She
            sometimes goes up to the fourth floor
            where the canteen is but no, I never go
            to the canteen because people always
            look at you, sitting on your own and think
            that you don't want to be on your own,
            when in fact you do want to be on your
            own and they get embarrassed and I
            don't like to see that, so I don't eat in the
            canteen. I eat my sandwiches elsewhere.
            Mmmm..
            [Blackout]

Smith does exercises.
[Blackout]

Smith: *[Washing from bucket]* No, I don't get
            telephone calls very often, but of all the
            calls that I don't get, she rings me the
            least, that is she probably does ring me,
            well of course she rings me, it's just that
            I'm never in you see, because I'm always
            doing things. I'm a busy person but I
            don't think that's a bad thing because if
            when she does ring and I'm not in she'll
            just think that I'm doing something
            important, which I am doing and she'll
            understand. No I don't think it can be a
            bad thing...

[Blackout]

Smith pushes table.
[Blackout]

Failing to sleep, trying to block out noise.
Sitting with walkman on in middle of room, back to audience.
[Blackout]

Climbing onto and jumping from chair.
Lying on floor. Leap up. Grab file. Go to door.
Remember jacket. Grab jacket and bowler hat.
Realise hat is in hand, return it. Deliberately pricking self on cactus. Glance out of window.
Rush to exit, fail to open door.
[Blackout]

Fifth Cycle.

Enter.
Make sure door is locked, confused that room is in wrong arrangement.
Move to where table should be and jacket should be, put jacket down.
Stand by window, close eyes. Re-run entry reoriented so desk is in correct place. Go to take off jacket but due to reorientation the chair is in the wrong place. Don't take off jacket, instead do it up high and turn up shirt collar.
[Blackout]

Smith: *[whilst pricking the palm of his hand with cactus]* When she did ring I was out, I had something or other that needed attending to, so she couldn't, wanted to ask me but *[pricks hand with cactus]*. Hello I said, didn't recognise her at first,

did I want to do something? No, no, no I
can't, too busy always *[pricks hand with
cactus]*. Others, second floor people,
hanging around. Mmm do something.
No, can't, busy, maybe one day *[pricks
hand hard with cactus]*.

Standing at medicine cabinet.
Listening at door.
Rubbing self with dry soap.
[Blackout]

Standing at window.
Sleeping on table with file, curled up.
Moving from piano to door with bowler hat on.
Do not exit. Bolt and chain door.
[Blackout]

Lights cross fade as Smith turns, looks at room and
smiles like Satie.
[Blackout]

Part 2

Voice: Erik never wrote poetry, he never took snapshots at the beach, listened to James Brown or stuffed hankies down his trousers. Erik never cooked lasagne, never ate curry, never threw up in the street. He never saw *Brief Encounter* never went skiing and never begged for bread. He never played netball, never had a bank account and never hit a kid.

                 Satie would never tell us about his life, his autobiography is nothing but a shopping list of lies. He said he always went to bed at 10.34, I know this isn't true. Satie never told us his thoughts but I can read them just the same.

The Treasures

Smith dressed as Satie is sitting at the desk facing the audience. He has a little portable cassette player on which he plays a recording he has made of himself asking questions, which are interspersed with silences. He switches on the table lamp to illuminate the cassette player and a bit of his face. He sometimes leans close to inspect the tape and its counter, other times he leans back and pretends to be Satie.

Tape: Good evening Mr. Satie.

Smith: Good evening.

Tape: There is one thing I have always wanted to ask.

Smith: Ask away.

Tape: Could you tell us about your childhood?

Smith: Yes.

Tape: Well tell us, when were you born?

Smith: I came very young into a world that was very old. Yes, I was born aged two.

Tape: Really, how interesting! At what age did you decide to be come a musician?

Smith: A musician? Don't be absurd, I never have and never will be a musician. I am a phonometrician. I measure sounds. On my phono-scale a common or garden F sharp measured 93 kilos, it came out of a fat tenor, whom I also weighed and yes, thank you. Thank you very much.

           [Waits a short while for the next question]

Tape: How is it that we only know of you as a musician?

Smith: I know it is so tiresome... I have many / plenty of enemies, loyal enemies. You might call them 'critics'.

           [Waits a short while for the next question]

Tape: Do you have any hobbies?

Smith: Yes.. yes.. oh yes! I collect black umbrellas and have over fifty, and I also have a large collec/

Tape: Fifty, how can you possibly use them all?

Smith: *[cursing his timing error]* Use them? That
          would be ridiculous! I keep them in my
          room out of the damp. And I also collect
          handkerchiefs, I have over a hundred
          now.

Tape: Presumably you don't use these
          handkerchiefs?

Smith: No, no I don't.

          *[Very long pause. When the interviewer
          finally speaks it is after a laugh]*

Tape: Mr. Satie tell us, do you still see Miss.
          Valadon ever?

Smith: Umm.. well... now and again, I suppose.

On the 14th of January, 1893 my love affair with Suzann Valadon began. It ended on Tuesday 20th of June.

Love is a sickness of the nerves. It is serious, yes, very serious. Myself, I'm afraid of it.

[Interrupting that reply]

Tape: You think love is a sickness?

Smith: Yes.. no.. I no, I yes. I find it very comical.

[Interrupting that reply]

Tape: Tell us about your day Mr. Satie.

Smith: Right yes. I wake up very early um, regularly very early at 7.18 and am inside, no and am inspired 10.23 to 11.47

[Interrupting that reply]

Tape: How would you describe yourself?

Smith: Umm right.. Hair: very little, grey and wispy, eyes grey (probably cloudy)... umm I'm sorry I can't give you my fingerprints, but I don't have them on me.

Tape: Do you like animals?

Smith: What is man doing to improve the mental condition of his fellow creatures? He offers them such a bad education that even a child would not choose it for itself.

Tape: What do you think about when you walk
             home late at night?

Smith: I um... think of the...

Tape: Where does your mind wander after
             you've had a drink?

As the difficult questions continue, Smith, troubled,
notices an imperfection on the wall. He picks up
white paint and a brush, turns on the room light,
picks at the wall paper, pulling off strips and sticking
them back with paint, obsessively.

Desespoire Agréable (Kyrie 1) is played on the
piano.

Tape: Who do you pray to?
             What do you say?
             What's the thought you've never let
             yourself think?
             When you talk to yourself? Who is
             listening?
             What do you still wish you had had the
             guts to do?

Music ends. Bright lights come up on stage. Smith
pretends to show people around his room.

Smith: ...so after that I decided I wanted to find
             out more about him.

             As a hobby? Well it's so much more than
             that, but yes. It is unusual I suppose. It
             does take up a lot of my time and
             prevents me getting out as much as I'd
             like, but people respect my dedication
             I'm sure.

Well they say they've never even heard of
him but I tell them they'd recognise his
stuff, his music, instantly.

Here's a final touch of paint. It's nearly
done. Yes it's all my own work, I'm quite
handy round the house. I've done it out
just the way that Satie's room would have
been. The dimensions are exactly similar.
The walls are white as you can see, door,
window, ceiling and the desk, the desk
where he would have written his music,
unless of course he wrote it at the piano (I
don't really know) probably both.
Anyway, if he'd written it at the desk it
would have been here, but if he wrote it
at the piano it would have been there;
except the piano's supposed to be there
but, well the floorboards are a bit
suspect. Yes, it should be there but I
don't really think that ...

*[Smith has difficulty persuading himself
that this discrepancy does not matter]*

Smith: Of course Erik's bedsit was on the second
            floor, though this is obviously just on the
            first you still get some sense of the uh...
            [Gestures altitude – hesitation]

Voice: Have you ever known when to stop?
            What wish would you make if you knew it
            would never come true?

Smith: Yes, I know it will be difficult to gain the
            status of a proper entrance fee museum. I
            have applied a couple of times but... but
            I don't know, facilities etc., you know,

shared bathroom, mmm...

Voice: How would you like to be remembered
             once you are dead?
             Who is the person closest to you?
             What do they know of you?

As the fiction has been breaking down more of the
awkward questions have been played over the
speakers. The lights have dimmed. The questions
continue until Smith has gathered himself. They
then stop and the lights come up. He is pretending
to be on television.

Smith: Right, if you set it up there we'll have me
             coming through the door.

             Good morning. Today we are in the
             home of Eric Smith, which houses what is
             probably the most comprehensive
             collection of Satie memorabilia anywhere.
             It is the remarkable result of a lifetime's
             dedication. We have with us today the
             eminent French musicologist Andre La
             Fontaine and he's going to tell us a little
             about Erik Satie. Andre...

Smith plays the French Musicologist talking in cod
French, then he returns to being the presenter.

Smith: Ah oui, M. Satie c'est un musicien... a tres
             bien c'est err Francais. Oui merci.

             Thank you very much Andre and now
             with no more ado, over to the man
             himself, Eric Smith.

             Thank you. There's so much here I want

to show you I don't know where to start.
[Looking at the birdcage he is holding]
This? Oh this is Satie's birdcage. I picked
it up at a second hand charity shop. This
bird does sing but needs plenty of
encouragement. Satie would probably
have had a linnet rather than a
nightingale. They migrate from North
Africa through the Carmargue.

Smith is drifting a bit, indicates furry hat on the floor.

Smith: There's my cat as well, it sits there. I'm
            hoping to turn the whole room into a
            museum and get it transported to Arcueil
            where Satie lived. I made this cabinet
            specially to display the smaller items and
            I'm going to build another cabinet here
            to make it look nice. The cabinet was
            made out of old wine packing cases,
            French wine of course.

Once more Smith has amused himself, he moves
the desk to under the cabinet.

Smith: I'm not sure what I'm going to make the
            big cabinet out of, maybe an old piano,
            with the hinge along here so it opens up.
            It's going to have three sort of places for
            pictures here. Satie liked threes, he was
            very spiritual and he drank lots of spirits.

Smith is very easily amused. He takes the three desk
draws out and stands them on end on top of the
desk, white undersides facing the audience.

Smith: Anyway, these are going to have lights
            here which sort of shine up and I thought

Picasso's cartoon of Satie could go in this
one, maybe a nice touch would be to
have Man Ray's photo in this one and in
the middle I've got a portrait of Socrates,
he was Satie's hero, I've got that
somewhere and that will go in the middle
- he dedicated his masterpiece to
Socrates. Then, if I could get it of course,
Valadon's portrait of Satie would hang on
this wall, opposite the door so as people
come in the door it's the first thing they
see.

Now I'd like to show you my treasures, if I
may. There's so much I want to show you.

The tone has become more intimate, almost as if he
were showing Suzanne these things.

Smith: *[Letters]* Oh, you'll like these. These are
                Satie's letters that he received from his
                girlfriend; she was called Suzanne. She
                was the painter *[gestures to fictional
                painting]*. He never opened any of his
                letters so they're sort of fascinating,
                nobody knows what they say or anything
                so it's all a mystery. I picked them up at
                an auction quite by chance in 1989,
                they're very valuable and postmarked.
                No, I've never wanted to open them. I
                think that would be rude.

                [Door Handle] And this, there's a great
                story to this. I was lucky enough to find it
                in a skip when I caught them demolishing
                Satie's tenement and, well that's it. He
                would have touched this twice a day, at
                least, four times if he had gone to the

shops, maybe not at all if he had been ill and didn't go out at all… anyway, it's made of solid brass. It's quite beautiful and is one of my favourites.

The cataloguing of his treasures is almost out to the audience.

Smith: *[Soap]* This is a piece of pumice he washed with.

[Ticket] And a bus ticket. Montmartre to Arcueil. Satie walked everywhere it's true but once it rained and if he'd forgotten his umbrella…

[Crushed tin can] This is the programme from the recitals given by his friend Ravel, he was a composer as well.

[Flaccid balloon] This is his swimming hat.

[Matchbox] These are his umbrellas. There are about forty there.

[Knife. He says nothing, just shows it]

I've got his glasses but they're on loan to the Prado, in Venice.

I've got all the gear, yes. Sometimes I wear it in the street. It seems to amuse people.

Smith shows off his Satie walk. Difficult questions play. The lights have dimmed. He arranges the treasures and admires them in the shrine.

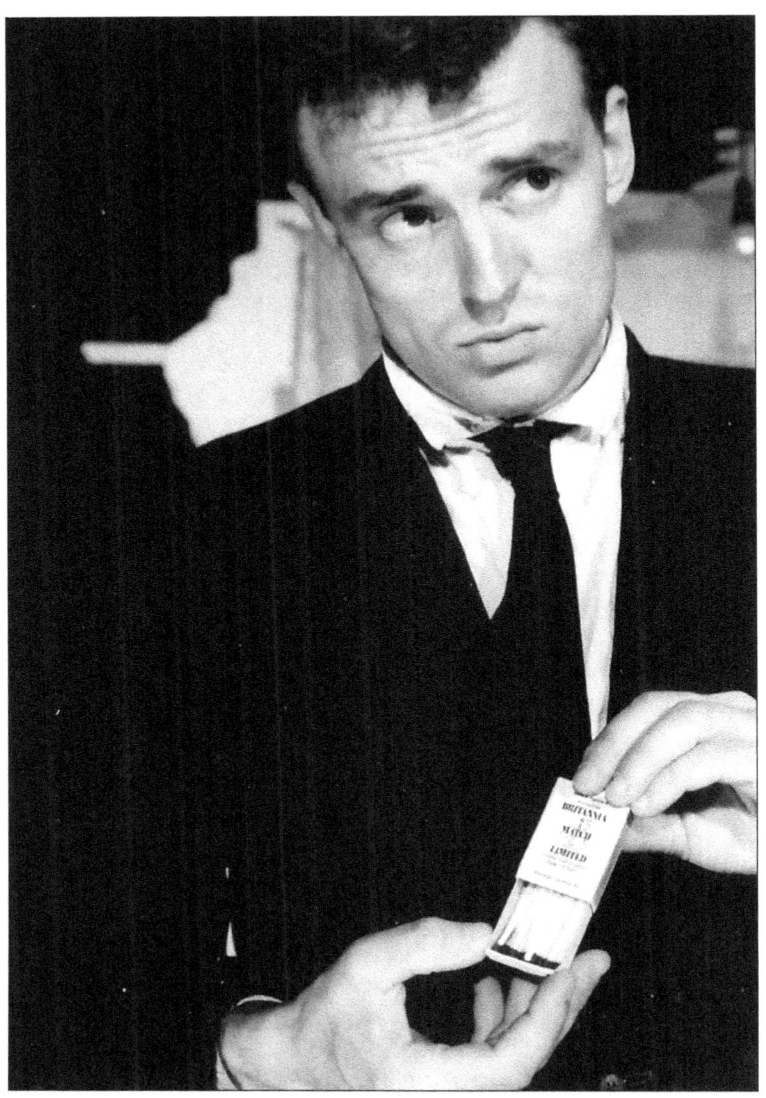
BRITANNIA
MATCH
LIMITED

Voice: What would you dream if you had a
            choice?
            Who are you now?
            Can you remember the last time you let
            yourself go?
            If you could have it all over again, is there
            really nothing you would change?
            When do you know what not to say?
            Do you say what you think? Always?

Desespoire Agréable (Kyrie II Choral) over the
speakers mixed with the questions.

As the questions come in Smith stares at his shrine
and sets up a Super 8 projector focussed on the
undersides of the draws. He turns the table lamp on
himself and provides a commentary to the film.

The film shows Smith dressed as Satie with a cotton
wool beard walking through Birmingham.

Smith: There is something else I would like to
            show you. This is some footage of Satie I
            have been lucky enough to get hold of.

            *[Smith putting money into collecting tin
            held by someone in a pink rabbit
            costume]*

Smith: Now can you spot the strange character
            in this shot? Yes that's right the pink
            rabbit there. This is a charity film. Yes
            that's right, this was shot by the Arcueil
            Save the Children Fund. That's one of
            their collectors and that there is Erik
            Satie. Now, he lived all his life in great
            poverty but he still manages to find a few
            centimes for the children. Erik loved

children and he used to organise trips to the beach for the poor ones where he lived, so I rooted around and managed to find this.

[Smith watching children at a fair]

Smith: Yes, genuine footage of Erik with his children at the seaside. You can see how happy they are and how happy he is, excellent.

[Smith walking past the Jesus Army]

Smith: Now this is a clip from a 1908 edition of *Songs of Praise*, this as you can see is Notre Dame, these are the Rosicrucians doing a song and dance number. Erik was a member of their sect but as you can see there, he just walks past them, they fell out and he later formed his own church.

[Smith going into Wimpy]

Smith: And this is footage of the gala opening of this cafe. Satie played piano here every Tuesday, Wednesday and Thursday. That was him going in and that was a celebrity pulling up in a taxi.

[Smith outside Birmingham Town Hall]

Smith: Now this next one is brilliant. A tourist on holiday in Athens, with a home movie camera. There's the Parthenon and who do they see outside? Could it be? Yes it is, it's our man Erik. Well they were obviously fans but Erik was ever so shy and there we go, running away and in a minute you see him covering his face. There! Excellent! Despite his years he can run very, very fast and easily outpaces my friend.

[Smith sitting on a park bench is included in a panning shot of a couple walking along together]

Smith: Now this, you'll all recognise this. *Last Tango in Paris,* classic neorealism, shooting in the street. There's Marlon Brando, Maria Schneider and who is that sitting on the bench? Yes, Mr Satie! He probably didn't even realise he was being filmed.

[Smith jumping on a parapet and bouncing on top of a multi-storey car park]

Smith: Finally, the only time Satie actually performed for the camera. This is Rene Clair's *Entr'acte,* a scene where Satie and Picabia, well Picabia isn't actually in it, but they jump from this cannon and bounce around and... then *[Reversing the projector back and forth]* does it backwards, isn't that amazing! It's more difficult than it looks but I can do it, I can do it!

Voice: What's the thought you've never let yourself think?
Have you ever thought of killing someone to make them yours?
Do you say what you think? Always?

Will you ever stop asking yourself
questions?

Insisting that he can do the jumping, Smith turns off
the projector. The questions have returned. Lights
come up to show Smith silhouetted jumping
forwards off and backwards onto a chair.

Despoire Agreable (Kyrie III Organ) plays over the
speakers.

[Back out]

Voice: There is this bird which sings outside my
                window, its tune is without interest and
                does not lend itself to orchestration.
                Though it practises continually it never
                improves.

Que Diras Tu plays over the speakers.

                In the mornings I can smell croissants and
                garlic wafting up from the street. I must
                always begin composing before the cafe's
                open otherwise their music distracts me
                and pop tunes keep sneaking into my
                work. I always keep my window closed to
                keep out the traffic fumes and noise. You
                can't write with someone else's melody
                stuck in your head.

Les Anges

In the blackness Smith dismantles the shrine and
rearranges the room so the table is end on against
the wall. This rearranging is not done quietly, the
noises of the activity compliment the soundtrack.

Lights fade up and down on a series of tableaux.

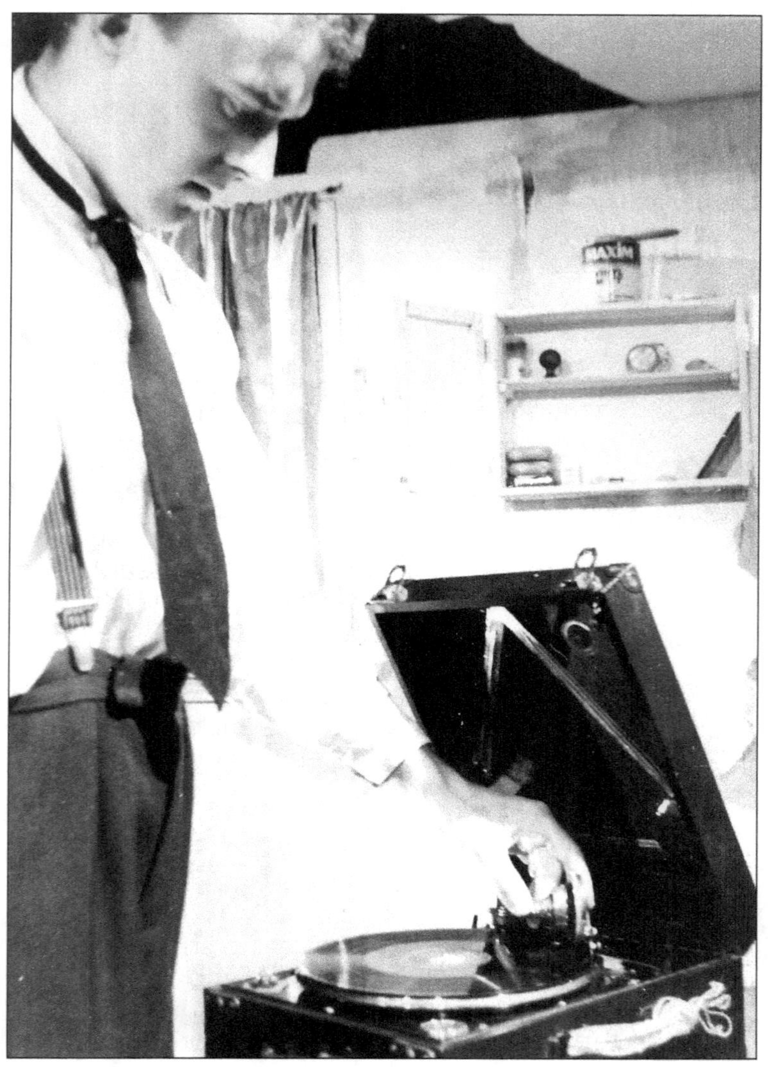

Smith sitting on desk reading a travel brochure which he throws away. *[Blackout]*

Smith does facial exercises and swings around so legs hang off desk. *[Blackout]*

Smith sits on desk back to audience, looks up to stage right. *[Blackout]*

The lights come up as Smith carries a gramophone to the desk and sets it up. *Que Diras Tu* finishes and the lights swell once more as a Linguaphone record starts calling out vowel sounds. Smith repeats the vowel sounds, in searching for the correct pronunciation he develops physical gestures for each sound. He builds these sounds to form simple sentences. *Vowels models 1,2,3 and 5* play in the pauses and under Smith's practising.

The telephone ringing interrupts his frustration. A similar panic to the first ringing. He carries the phone to the desk and answers it. To his horror all that he can say are a series of guttural noises related to the vowel sounds.

The person at the other end has hung up.

Disappointed Smith closes his eyes to re-run the call. The phone starts ringing. This conversation could be just him playing at being called up. He speaks too much for there to really be someone at the other end.

Smith: ...Hello? Speaking, Eric Smith. No, I'm sure you've got the right one. That wasn't me, somebody else probably. And you are? Oh Suzanne, from work! Yes, we chatted/ spoke/ acknowledged each other on the stairwell once. Of course I remember. No I don't mind being rung up at this time. Yes, I'm not busy, not like usual anyway. Tomorrow? Not sure, very busy on a Friday. You'd like to meet me in the park? Well I'm not sure. Seven o'clock would be fine for you? Oh, I think that's fine for me too. But won't your friends from the second floor...? What? You've never liked them? And only ever really liked me? Right, I see. Seven at the park, yes, see you there then. Suits me fine. Yes, goodbye. Mmm, bye then, bye. Yes I feel the same way. Bye bye.

In a haze Smith picks up the phone once more to see if she is still there. To his surprise there is the voice of *Les Anges* singing. He looks up confused and sees light pouring through the window. Amazed he climbs over the desk to investigate.

Les Anges plays over the speakers.

Moving the cactus to avoid being pricked Smith gently strokes the curtains, runs his hand tentatively between them before parting them and hooking them up. The moment he starts opening the curtains the solo voice of *Les Anges* is supplemented with seedy jazz piano, saxophone and bass.

The star mobile is glinting and Smith is like a kid, he counts the stars, gazes at them, his breath condenses on the window. His hand strays to the latch and he opens the window to see the stars more clearly. Yet as he opens the window the stars disappear. Smith is confused and looks around as a cartoon character would. He closes the window and

is shocked to see the stars back. He repeats
opening and closing the window until he works out
what is happening. In disgust he closes the curtains.

Les Anges has finished.

Severe Reprimand is played live.

Smith angry with himself, unplugs the telephone and coils the flex around the receiver and puts it in the pile of rubbish. He finds the soap and the scene ends with Smith frantically rubbing the skin on the back of his neck with the bar of dried soap.

[Blackout]

The Piano

Vexations is played on the piano.

Light comes up on Smith in full Satie gear sitting at the desk, his back to the piano. On his right is a huge mound of paper. He is drawing in staves on the sheet in front of him. When he gets to the bottom he carefully places this sheet on top of all the others. Massages his fingers. Moves the pile to his left. Takes the top sheet off. Squares it in front of himself and prepares to compose.

Composing is more difficult than Smith had anticipated. He rearranges the various objects in front of him in the hope that their ordering will hold the key to his inspiration. He tries making sounds from the objects in his search for the opening note, including his squeal when pricked by the cactus. All sounds are unsatisfactory. The bird does not sing for him. He tries dropping his pen on the paper, this gives a note, very low. He tries more random notes, the tune is virtually un-performable and definitely not easy to listen to. Smith would be happy with his efforts but at each stage he becomes aware of the pianist playing *Vexations*. Eventually they confront each other, Pianist takes his music and leaves.

Confronted for the first time by the piano Smith is nervous of playing any notes. Eventually he finds a random note and octave span which pleases him, it corresponds to the width of his manuscript. He takes his random notes on his fingers and transfers them to the piano. It is an unpromising chord but Smith is happy. He thinks about adding a left hand but decides against it. He likes the chord and wants to commit it to paper, then realises the paper is well out of reach. He tries stretching, using absurd techniques to help him get close whilst keeping his fingers on the chord. The pianist returns and takes over the chord. Smith thinks he is helping and starts to scribble down the notes. Pianist however uses the chord as a start for an improvisation.

The noise of the piano is driving into Smith's brain. There follows a passage of improvisation in which Pianist, Actor and Lighting Operator all play off each other, using motifs from other points in the show, building up atmospheres and microscopic logics. The improvisation wil finish with the actor spinning in circles with his eyes closed, Walkman on full blast he will stagger to a halt. The lights will be the last element quelled, giving the room its own independent existence.
[Blackout]

Nocturn 5 is played on the piano.

Smith begins setting up the stage for the final part.

Part 3: The Death of Socrates

After *Nocturn* has finished and Pianist left, the blackout continues as the stage is being set.

Elegy plays over the speakers.

Voice: Now I catch my mind failing, I feel the bindings coming loose. Now I know I'm scared and with the fear come questions, questions and prayers.

I look at my edited history and question its colour. Until this failing I had the clarity to censor my life but it has taken its toll, cost me my strength, taken my strength and given me strength.

I just pray I can hold it all together to the end.
Please to God when the end is close don't let me give myself up and throw it all away.
Please to God I can finish safe inside my story.
Please to God I will die with my hat on, umbrella in hand.

The lights come up. Smith has set up the whole room as a shrine with a place for himself on a chair on top of the desk at its centre. All the props are displayed. Smith's suit and shirt are part of the shrine. He is putting on a long newspaper toga.

Socrate One plays over the speakers.

Voice: What happens when you can't find the edge of your sm le and you've grown inside your clothes so the black cloth is your skin and this hat is your skull? What happens when your suit leaves you naked and you must wear a coat to hide your shame? What happens when you look at yourself in the mirror and only see what everyone else sees?

What do you do when you see the end of your story coming up on and you don't like its shape? How do you change a story you've already published? Now that I have set down my plot I must follow it to its conclusion. I decided how it was to be written and how I was to be read and such as is written, so shall it be, so help me God.

Our story has been brought to the point where something has to happen. We have become entwined to the point where nothing can separate us. I can't move without giving you up. I have to give you up but giving you up is not enough. There have to be ways of pulling in a new purity. There must be strategies for wiping your head clean, scrubbing out the pollution of you.

I've asked myself what happens when a hero takes on too much, starts getting in the way, hurts as much as he helps? What do you do with a hero you cannot touch, whose world you can't enter? How do you impose yourself on their story, write yourself into their life? Once you have taken your passion so far you must take it further, you must make a permanent attachment.

You know more about them than it is possible without destiny intervening, there is no doubt that destiny is involved, no doubt on the next page your two paths will join. They do not know you exist but soon all that will change. Soon you will be forever entwined. Soon you will be fused.

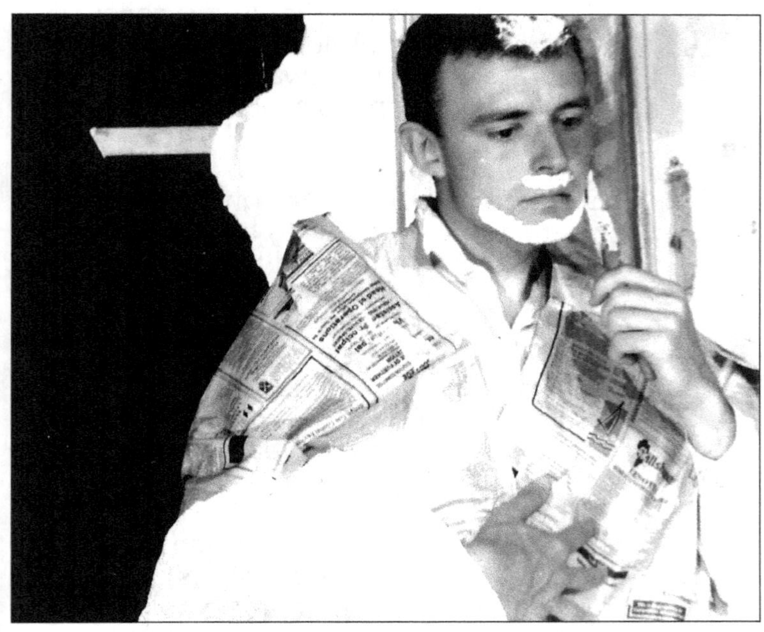

Smith has used emulsion that once painted the wall to now paint his hair white and a beard on his chin. He adds cotton wool to the paint. He sets the gramophone needle on *Morte De Socrate* on an old record player. The projector runs the documentary film backwards. Lights fade so only the room practical and table lamp show. Smith uses the table lamp to light himself as he acts out The Death Of Socrates, allowing silences for the absent performers to say their lines. The acting is poor but moving nonetheless.

Smith: Friends, all, I thank you for your kindness, your flattery does me proud.

There's someone at the door. The jailer. Let him in but tempt him not with your bribes, nor return evil for what you see as an evil done unto us.

Welcome jailer.

You are too kind, but let fate take its course. I know you're only doing your job. Do not delay in administering the poison, it only prolongs the sorrow of my friends.

What a charming fellow.

And um how should I take this stuff?

Right, and may I spill some as an oblation to the Gods?

Oh, fair enough. You're the expert. I thank you.

Now I shall pray to the gods to ask for a
safe journey. Gods, please give me a safe
journey. I would give you some of this but
there's only just enough.

Right, down the hatch.

Now I just walk around a bit?

How good it is to be with friends and to
discuss good philosophy at the end. But
friends, why are you crying? Shed not
your tears, I had to send Plato out coz I
knew he would blub.

Oh, I think you're right, it's working.

[Smith climbs onto his chair on the desk]

I can't feel my toes anymore or my feet.
My legs are gone, it's spreading.
When it reaches my heart I know I'll be a
goner. My hips. Crito, Crito, one last
thing before I go... remember to...

Socrates is about to say his last words sitting in the
middle of the shrine when he notices the record is
jumping and will never end.

There is a slow fade to black.

Voice: How can I ever know you, him, anyone?
            How can I read the texts of your passing?
            How can I tease from this filigree the
            days, the minutes, the long years of your
            life? What can fill the gaps and who am I
            to believe? You tell me you are no hero
            but maybe I know better.

There are those who say they know you,
but still laugh at you.
There are those who talk about you, but
only tell of themselves.
There are the outsiders, who take you as
you let them find you.
There is no intimacy, no compassion.
You are their next subject and a simple
story.

The final tableau is the shrine without Smith in it.
Fairy lights are round the window and medicine
cabinet, light comes through the window and the
door which is open on its chain.

Epilogue Elegy plays over the speakers.

In the place of the final missing chord come the
house lights.

Original Programme Notes

Memoirs of an Amnesiac

"Bring Black Glasses and Something
to Plug Your Ears With"
Relâche 1924

Erik Satie was born in Honfleur, France
on 19 May 1866.
He composed music.
He died in Paris, France on 1 July 1925.
This is his biography,
some of it is true.

Part 1
The Room

Part 2
The Treasures
Les Anges
The Piano

Part 3
The Death of Socrates

Devised by Richard Chew, Graeme Rose
and James Yarker

Performed by Graeme Rose and Richard Chew

Music by Erik Satie and Richard Chew

All Design, Construction and Operation
by Stan's Cafe

<u>Voices</u>
Soprano: Rosalind Martin
Mezzo: Cheryl Pickering
Tenor: Howard Kirk
Baritone: Mark Griffiths
Bass: Richard Chew
Speaker: Francois Descarts

Thank You
To the huge number of people without whose help
and understanding this show could never have been
made, you know who you are.

Studio recording was made possible with the
financial assistance of St. Giles Cripplegate

Making Memoirs: A Conversation

In January 2020 founding members of Stan's Cafe, Graeme Rose and James Yarker look back 28 years on the making of their second show.

James: You and Rick [Richard Chew] had been talking about making a piece about Erik Satie together before Stan's Cafe was formed, hadn't you?

Graeme: Yes, at Lancaster University Pete Brooks had staged a Dada-inspired performance event with members of Welfare State called *The White Buffet* and Pete asked me to take the role of Satie – I just sat at a table looking enigmatic. I remember you pulled a plucked supermarket chicken across the stage on a leash.

James: I don't remember that at all! I remember doing something with Ursula [Martinez] involving our hair and spaghetti.

Graeme: That's right! After that Rick and I talked about our mutual love of [Satie's] music and writings and persona. We loved his rich, dry humour. There is a heartbreaking story about Satie's apartment: after he died Darius Milhaud and his wife Madelaine took on responsibility for sorting it out. No one had been inside before and they found rows of identical clothing, dozens of umbrellas and a stack of unsent letters written to Suzanne Valadon; two pianos, one completely covered in papers, but the flat was also incredibly spartan, a wooden chair, a hard bed and little else. No one knew about his personal life, whether he had a lover, or anybody. He was clearly a local legend as in Arcueil each year he would take local kids to the seaside, so at his funeral the cortege was followed by hundreds of kids.

James: I'd forgotten how much biographical detail we'd got into the show. It turns out lots of those strange performance details were just us reproducing Satie!

Graeme: I'd found a 12" vinyl recording of Simon Rattle conducting Satie from what must have been the mid 70s. it included an extract from *Relâche*, plus a version of *Socrate* for voice and piano.

James: And we went to see the film *Entr'acte*, from *Relâche*, at the French institute.

Graeme: Yes, that was September 26th, 1991; we bumped into Lois Keidan and a year later we were at the ICA performing the show.

James: Really, that screening was before we'd made *Perry Como['s Christmas Cracker]*?

Graeme: It was really early. We were inspired by how they played with time in that film. We lifted a moment from it when Satie and Francis Picabia jump from a ledge onto a roof and then reverse that backwards and forward.

James: And Socrate came in at the end of the show.

Graeme: We had been exploring the fascination with the cult of personality, perhaps. The idea of a hero; how you look up at them and ultimately may have to destroy them. A key filmic reference you introduced us to was Scorsese's *The King Of Comedy* and those 1950's audio recordings of Gerard Hoffnüng, in which he mythologises himself. We started to speculate that maybe Satie idolised Socrates.

James: At the start I was very worried about you just pretending to be Satie. That's why we introduced Eric Smith as a kind of buffer and I always enjoyed the fact that by the end of the show it was possible to see you playing Smith playing Satie playing Socrates.

Graeme: Your discipline in that really helped. It may feel like an obvious thing now but back then it may not have seemed so, it was the perfect way of accessing the material through the lens of our position at the time.

James: I remember it being quite intense and personal.

Graeme: It was. It was about us working out our methodology by doing and finding. We immersed ourselves in music and work and writing and with a playful exploration of ideas. Satie's spartan apartment mirrored our own physical circumstances. We introduced the idea of a love interest and that in some way was a rendering of our own situation.

James: I thought that was just me. What a relief!

Graeme: Satie allowed us to visit a sense of the exotic so we could slip from the mundane to a more continental reality. We attempted to explore the French vowel sounds.

James: That was because our friend Maggie had that beautiful old wind-up gramophone. We had to get that into the show and it had those crazy language discs with it.

Graeme: They played at 78rpm and were extraordinary.

James: I remember you had been on a workshop with Station House Opera and brought some of their thinking to the show.

Graeme: That's right. Julian Maynard Smith would set up a sequence and then change one small element of that sequence, and from that one small disruption the logic unravels. We used that in the early 'daily-routine' sequence.

James: And the editing of time into small visual phrases using blackouts was an old glory what glory device.

Graeme: We [(glory what glory)] perhaps became slave to that technique but it worked really well for us in *Memoirs*. It allowed us to be playful with a filmic language that showed routine and the perception of time passing. We wanted to draw attention to, and elevate the idea of the mundane. You had just finished working in that office in Reading.

James: And you worked for a bit in the Northfield Department of Social Security.

Graeme: We were able to share some of that office experience.

James: We got the set off Sam Mason.

Graeme: Yes, he was teaching at a school in Chelmsley Wood and got cast-off set from Pebble Mill [TV studios]. We used some of that. I remember when we first packed the tour van we had to saw off the excess bits so we could close the doors before driving off!

James: You'd been inspired for the set by Steve Shill?

Graeme: I'd seen his show *A Fine Film Of Ashes* in about 1988 which had this corruption of a classic drawing room set, and you could clearly see the edges, the margins of it, so it was very self-consciously a constructed set. We were interested in the fakery of the set coming to life somehow.

James: That explains the shift in lighting states that open and close the show. There was probably some Forced Entertainment in there somewhere as well?

Graeme: I think being able to penetrate through the layers of fiction very easily comes from them. It felt very satisfying in performance, to play those levels of fiction against each other. Bathos undermining the pomposity.

James: I'd read Cocteau, *Les Enfants Terribles* and the idea for The Treasures came from that, and then, for me, presenting one thing as another is related to that Magritte painting, *This Is Not A Pipe*.

Graeme: It's like the fiction is happening inside the mind of the character, but how far are the audience going to be drawn into believing it? There's a fragile grasp on reality and if you buy into it you are potentially putting yourself in some kind of peril.

James: Looked at now you'd be identifying Smith with Asperger's or Autism Spectrum Disorder or something?

Graeme: Yes, in the contemporary world we'd think more about the mental health dimension. Eric Smith is a loner, who appears at times to be delusional, who gets sucked into his own layers of fiction and ends up believing in his own myth. This relates to Rupert Pupkin from *The King of Comedy* and the degree to which he is deluded by his obsession with his hero Jerry Lewis. You know it's not going to end well! Compare this with Joachim Phoenix in *The Joker*, which I think owes a great debt to this film.

You were demanding the material didn't take an obvious route, that it took an alternative standpoint, and that helped us look at it though a slightly different lens and ask more difficult questions about the material.

James: It was great working with Rick as well. I really felt I was facilitating you two make the show you were both desperate to make and utterly committed to.

Graeme: I remember us having free access to the Progress Theatre [in Reading] and doing a late one. We stayed late into the night to finish making the show, and the three of us were laughing so much, practically wetting ourselves we were enjoying it so much. It felt so rich and vital.

James: When I look at the Stan's Cafe back catalogue this is one of the few very early shows that I'd consider reviving.

Graeme: For me some shows are like love affairs, and *Memoirs* was the first piece that felt like a love affair. It got under my skin and I adored it. Of course, it helped that others liked it, but I knew that whatever the reaction was we'd made something very beautiful. I knew without a shadow of a doubt coming off stage that we'd nailed it.

About the illustration and design

The illustrations for the covers of these books were undertaken by students at Birmingham City University as the final module of their first-year illustration course during the Spring/Summer of 2018. The images were developed through workshops using variations of the theatre-devising methods employed by Stan's Cafe but adapted and applied to the making of visual work. The resulting work was shown in the pop-up exhibition *The Something Of Somebody Something* at Stan's Cafe's venue @AE Harris in May 2018.

The design concept of the books was produced by final year Graphic Design student Aimee Chapman. These were then further developed for print in a collaborative process between Stan's Cafe and the University's Innovation Product Support Service (IPSS) which involved helping the company to select appropriate DTP software, undertaking training and selecting a suitable print on demand service.

Gareth Courage
Lecturer in Illustration
Birmingham City University